Dinosaur Detectives
Search for the Facts...

Stegosaurus
and Other
Jurassic Dinosaurs

BROWN BEAR BOOKS

Published by Brown Bear Books Ltd
4877 N. Circulo Bujia
Tucson, AZ 85718
USA

and

Leroy House
436 Essex Rd
London N1 3QP
UK

© 2018 Brown Bear Books Ltd

ISBN 978-1-78121-406-0

Library of Congress Cataloging-in-Publication Data available on request

Text: Tracey Kelly
Designer: John Woolford
Design Manager: Keith Davis
Editorial Director: Lindsey Lowe
Children's Publisher: Anne O'Daly
Picture Manager: Sophie Mortimer

Picture Credits
Shutterstock: Alvita Arika 4

Brown Bear Books has made every attempt to contact the copyright holder.
If you have any information please contact: licensing@brownbearbooks.co.uk

Manufactured in the United States of America
CPSIA compliance information: Batch#AG/5609

Websites
The website addresses in this book were valid at the time of going to press. However, it is possible that contents or addresses may change following publication of this book. No responsibility for any such changes can be accepted by the author or the publisher. Readers should be supervised when they access the Internet.

Contents

How Do We Know about Dinosaurs?

Scientists are like detectives.

They look at dinosaur fossils.

Fossils tell us where dinosaurs lived.

They tell us how big they were.

Use your detective skills! Visit a natural history museum. You might see a dinosaur! This skeleton is *Stegosaurus*.

How to Use This Book

This tells you what the animal ate.

Plant-eater

Meat-eater

These tell you when the animal lived.

150 million years ago

JURASSIC PERIOD

Stegosaurus

(Say it!) (STEG-oh-SAWR-us)

Stegosaurus had blunt teeth.
It had big plates on its back.
These helped to protect it.
Its tail had sharp spikes, too!

Large plates along back

First found in ...
Colorado, 1877

FACT FILE

NAME: *Stegosaurus* means "roofed lizard"
WEIGHT: up to 5 tons (4.5 metric tons)
FOOD: plants
HABITAT: forests and grasslands

Humped back

MINI FACTS
Stegosaurus's brain was the size of a walnut!

Tail with spikes

How big am I?

30 ft (9 m)

Short front legs

Long back legs

20

21

This shows you how big the animal was.

A map shows where the first fossils were found.

Read on to become a dinosaur detective!

5

What Was Earth Like?

Stegosaurus lived in the Jurassic period.

That was 150 million years ago.

Trees and plants grew everywhere.

Dinosaurs walked the Earth.

And great reptiles flew in the sky.

Barapasaurus

Say it! **(ba-RAP-ah-SAWR-us)**

Barapasaurus was a giant plant-eater!
It pulled leaves from branches.
Then it swallowed them whole.

Teeth for tearing leaves

Long neck stretched up into trees

How big am I?

46 ft (14 m)

 **MINI FACTS**

Barapasaurus was a sauropod. Sauropods were huge. They had long necks and tails. They ate plants.

FACT FILE

NAME: *Barapasaurus* means "big legged lizard"

WEIGHT: 35 tons (32 metric tons)

FOOD: plants

HABITAT: plains

First found in ...
India, 1958

Long tail to balance body

9

Brachiosaurus

 Say it! (BRACK-ee-oh-SAWR-us)

Brachiosaurus was twice as tall as a giraffe!

It ate leaves high up in the treetops.

It had strong legs. They held its huge weight.

How big am I?

85 ft (26 m)

MINI FACTS

Brachiosaurus lived in small herds. The young stayed in the middle. That kept them safe.

It could reach trees
46 feet (14 m) high

FACT FILE

NAME: *Brachiosaurus* means "arm lizard"
WEIGHT: up to 60 tons (54 metric tons)
FOOD: leaves and twigs
HABITAT: wooded places

Long neck shaped
like a giraffe's

The front
legs were
longer
than the
back legs

First found in ...
Colorado, 1900

Compsognathus

Say it! (komp-SOG-nay-thus)

Compsognathus was a meat-eater. It was the weight of a chicken! It had a long neck and tail. This dinosaur could run very fast. It crept through the trees. Then it darted out to catch prey.

MINI FACTS

Dinosaurs laid eggs, like birds do. Scientists have found fossil eggs.

Long tail for balance

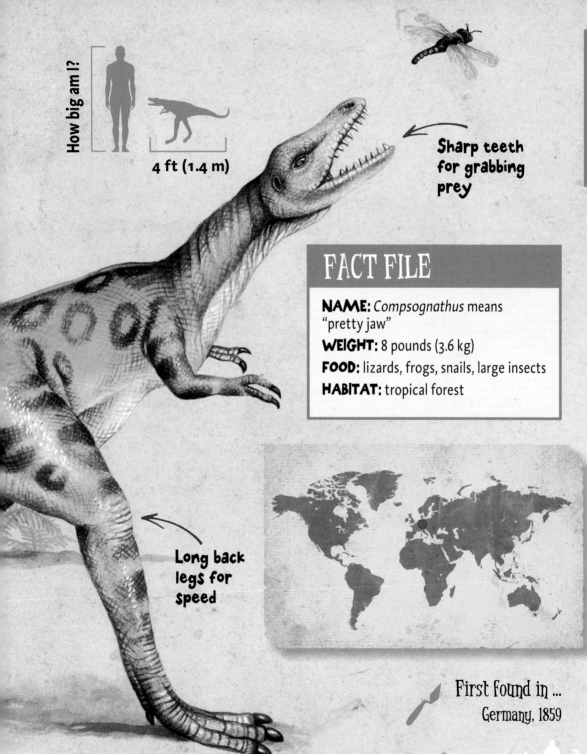

How big am I?

4 ft (1.4 m)

Sharp teeth
for grabbing
prey

FACT FILE

NAME: *Compsognathus* means
"pretty jaw"

WEIGHT: 8 pounds (3.6 kg)

FOOD: lizards, frogs, snails, large insects

HABITAT: tropical forest

Long back
legs for
speed

First found in ...
Germany, 1859

13

Megalosaurus

(Say it!) **(MEGG-ah-low-SAWR-us)**

Megalosaurus had a big head.

It had sharp claws to grab prey.

Megalosaurus was a meat-eater.

It could run fast over short distances.

Large body ➤

🐾 MINI FACTS

Megalosaurus killed other dinosaurs.
Then it ate them.
It ate dead animals, too.

How big am I?

26 ft (8 m)

Strong jaws
to kill prey

FACT FILE

NAME: *Megalosaurus* means
"great lizard"

WEIGHT: 1 ton (1 metric ton)

FOOD: other dinosaurs

HABITAT: near water

Walked on two
powerful legs

First found in ...
England, 1676

15

Seismosaurus

Say it! (SIZE-moe-SAWR-us)

Seismosaurus was very long! It had a long neck. Its teeth were shaped like pegs! They pulled leaves from branches to eat.

Very long body

Long tail for hitting enemies

How big am I?

110 ft (33 m)

 **MINI FACTS**

Seismosaurus was heavy. Its footsteps made the ground shake!

FACT FILE

NAME: *Seismosaurus* means "earthquake lizard"

WEIGHT: 30 tons (27 metric tons)

FOOD: leaves

HABITAT: deserts and lowlands

JURASSIC PERIOD

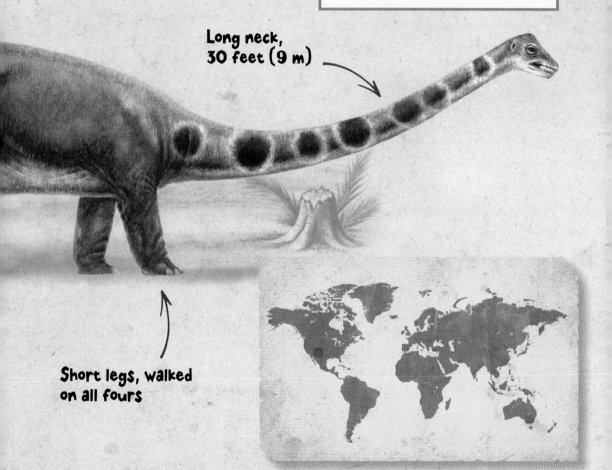

Long neck, 30 feet (9 m)

Short legs, walked on all fours

First found in ...
New Mexico, 1979

Shunosaurus

Say it! (shoo-NOH-zawr-us)

Shunosaurus was a small dinosaur.
It was a plant-eater. But it could fight
off enemies. *Shunosaurus* had a bony tail.
It could swing it to hit other dinosaurs.

How big am I?

33 feet (10 m)

🔍 MINI FACTS

Shunosaurus lived
in China. Scientists
found 20 whole
fossils there.

Bony club at the
end of its tail

Spoon-shaped teeth

FACT FILE

NAME: *Shunosaurus* means "Shu lizard"

WEIGHT: 3.3 tons (3 metric tons)

FOOD: plants

HABITAT: forests

First found in ...
China, 1977

Stegosaurus

(Say it!) **(STEG-oh-SAWR-us)**

Stegosaurus had blunt teeth.

It had big plates on its back.

These helped to protect it.

Its tail had sharp spikes, too!

FACT FILE

NAME: *Stegosaurus* means "roofed lizard"

WEIGHT: up to 5 tons (4.5 metric tons)

FOOD: plants

HABITAT: forests and grasslands

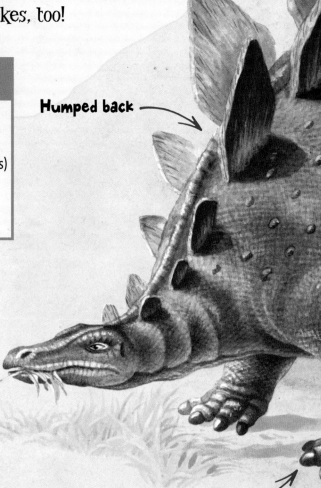

Humped back →

Short front legs →

How big am I?

30 ft (9 m)

Large plates
along back

First found in ...
Colorado, 1877

MINI FACTS

Stegosaurus's brain
was the size of a walnut!

Tail with spikes

Long back legs

Dinosaur Quiz

Test your dinosaur detective skills!
Can you answer these questions?
Look in the book for clues.
The answers are on page 24.

1 Whose skeleton is this?

2 Where did *Shunosaurus* live?

3 What did this dinosaur eat?

4 Which dinosaur made the ground shake when it walked?

Glossary

fossil
Part of an animal or plant in rock.
The animal or plant lived in ancient times.

habitat
The kind of place where an animal usually lives.

herd
A group of animals that lives together.

meat-eater
An animal that eats mostly meat.

plant-eater
An animal that eats only plants, not meat.

prey
An animal that is hunted
by other animals for food.

Find out More

Books

The Big Book of Dinosaurs,
DK Editors (DK Children, 2015)

Danger: Dinosaurs! (Jurassic World)
(Step into Reading), Courtney
Carbone (Random House, 2015)

Websites

discoverykids.com/category/
dinosaurs/

www.kids-dinosaurs.com/
brachiosaurus.html

www.newdinosaurs.com

Index

Quiz Answers 1. *Stegosaurus.* **2.** *Shunosaurus* lived in China. **3.** *Compsognathus* ate lizards, frogs, snails, and large insects. **4.** *Seismosaurus* made the Earth shake. It was very heavy!